TETBURY, NAILSWORTH AND MINCHINHAMPTON IN OLD PHOTOGRAPHS

TETBURY, NAILSWORTH AND MINCHINHAMPTON IN OLD PHOTOGRAPHS

COLLECTED BY
ALAN SUTTON

ALAN SUTTON
1988

Alan Sutton Publishing Limited
Brunswick Road · Gloucester

First published 1988

British Library Cataloguing in Publication Data

Tetbury, Nailsworth and Minchinhampton in old photographs.
1. Gloucestershire, history
I. Sutton, Alan, *1949–*
942.4′1

ISBN 0-86299-402-0

Front cover illustration: the junction of Church Street and Long Street, Tetbury. See page 24.

Pages 2 and 6, details from the Tetbury Coronation Celebrations, 1902. See page 43.

Typesetting and origination by
Alan Sutton Publishing Limited.
Printed in Great Britain by
WBC Print Limited, Bristol.

CONTENTS

INTRODUCTION

The area covered by this book is basically the historic hundred of Longtree. Hundreds were the administrative units of each county and date back to Saxon times, but they fell out of use and were replaced by other forms of local government before the end of the eighteenth century. In ancient times, the meeting place for representatives of Longtree Hundred was at Chavenage Green, where presumably the 'long' or tall tree stood. Today, the valley running down to Avening is still called Longtree Bottom. In the Middle Ages, the places of importance in Longtree Hundred were Minchinhampton and Tetbury but, by the eighteenth century, both of these towns were suffering economic decline. The opening of the new road from Bath to Gloucester in 1780, together with the cloth industry creating much employment in the valleys, made Nailsworth a more important centre. This was further emphasised by the coming of the railways. The Nailsworth branch opened in 1867 and, although Tetbury eventually obtained its branch line in 1889, it was too late to have a great economic effect. Minchinhampton, isolated on the hill, was not to have a line at all, although the town stood reasonably close to halts at Brimscombe and Chalford.

The wool trade has left its mark over most of the area covered by the photographs in this book. Tetbury and Minchinhampton were both important wool markets and even had some cloth manufacturing, though on a modest scale. The results of the success of this wool trade may be seen in the fine stone buildings that stand in these towns today. Nailsworth had a different pattern of development. It was originally a group of separate hamlets in the parishes of Avening, Horsley and Minchinhampton; but, through the eighteenth and nineteenth centuries, its importance increased and the hamlets grew into a town; formally recognised and defined as a civil parish as late as 1892. This different form of development shows and, unlike its hilltop neighbours, Nailsworth cannot boast great antiquity in its town centre.

The photographs of these three towns and some of the surrounding villages have been split into three sections. The layout is, by necessity rather arbitrary. Basically the layout is intended to form a journey, but this has not always been possible and some photographs have been placed where best suited, even if slightly out of a journey sequence. Because of the journey sequence, some photographs are far apart in the book notwithstanding geographic proximity. The best example of this is Watledge, (page 114) which is included in the Nailsworth sequence and Pinfarthings, just a fraction away up the hill, which is in the Minchinhampton sequence, between Box and Amberley (pages 162–3).

The photographs date from as early as the 1860s up to the 1960s, though mainly covering the three decades from 1890 to 1920; the golden age of picture postcards. It was during this thirty-year span that a complete industry developed, generating local views that could be used for quick inter-family messages before the telephone came into common usage. A typical message would read:

> *Shall be with you at 3p.m. tomorrow. Mabel will not come, she has a bad cold, just expect me and boys, love Ada.*

The penny post was reliable and with several collections and deliveries each day, could be used for messages that showed a surprising expectation of immediacy – that is, surprising to us being used to the 'progress' of the later twentieth century! Some cards are sent home from holidays, but the holidays are usually visiting relations in the area and often bear postscript messages such as 'I expect you recognise this. . .'.

Through this vast archive of images, we gain an impression of life some 80 years ago. We see that in this area at least, there were few trees; the hillsides are almost bare. We see vast areas of land that are now covered with houses and sites showing buildings long since gone. But, perhaps most evocative of all, we see our grandparents and great-grandparents when they were small children, for the people in these pictures are the essential ingredient that brings the book alive.

Alan Sutton
Hydefield
Uley

Another enlargement from the picture on page 43. The detail is amusing to investigate. The full picture shows the overall group scene, but when enlarged much more becomes apparent. Note the old boy, right at the back with a beard, surreptitiously helping himself from the barrel.

SECTION ONE

Tetbury

THE ROYAL AUSTRALIAN FLYING CORPS at Leighterton, 1914–18. These two pictures are both very faded and damaged, but are of great interest as so little is available on the aerodrome at Leighterton.

WESTONBIRT HOUSE, c. 1910. The house was built in 1870 by Robert Stayner Holford, on the site of the old manor house which he demolished in 1863. The estate was later sold to the Martyr's Memorial and Church of England Trust, and in 1928 the Trust established Westonbirt School, a girls public school.

THE NEW VILLAGE OF WESTONBIRT c. 1930. R.S. Holford had demolished most of the village cottages which lay on both sides of the Easton Grey road, and rebuilt them further west, most of the rebuilding being completed by 1856.

THE HARE AND HOUNDS HOTEL. Once a humble coaching inn, a quarter of mile from the present hotel on the old main road, the Hare and Hounds was demolished by R.S. Holford, and rebuilt on the present site in his usual grandiose style in 1854. The top picture was taken *c.* 1895, the bottom picture *c.* 1930.

BEVERSTONE CASTLE, two views of c. 1910.

CUCKOLD'S KNAPP, *c.* 1910. The National School is on the left-hand side, and Mrs Dance, the headmaster's wife (an extremely short woman) is standing outside the school house.

ST SAVIOUR'S CHURCH, *c.* 1905. Built as a chapel of ease in 1848 to the design of S.W. Daukes, it became redundant in 1976.

LONDON ROAD AND THE POLICE STATION at the corner of Long Street, *c.* 1905.

THE BOTTOM END OF LONG STREET, from approximately outside the Ferns *c.* 1895, showing the old council offices at Porch House. The houses on the immediate right were demolished for the new Methodist Hall in 1909.

THE ORMOND'S HEAD, c. 1880, doubling as the Midland Railway goods and parcels receiving office. Before Tetbury had its own station in 1889, both the Midland Railway and the Great Western Railway vied for parcel and goods trade. The GWR office was in the Market Place. Note the condition of the road at this time.

LONG STREET, *c.* 1935, the Ormond's Head showing the new façade, and Robert Street's garage, on the site of which Gateway now stands.

LONG STREET, *c.* 1930. This photograph is taken looking away from the market hall, with the garage shown more clearly.

LONG STREET. Two views, thirty years apart. The top picture, *c.* 1900 shows the Close Hotel centre left. This was built by John Seede around 1583, and sold shortly afterwards by his son to Thomas Estcourt. From the mid-seventeenth century until 1850 it was in the hands of the Savage family. The bottom picture dates from *c.* 1930, and was presumably taken on the same day as the picture on the preceding page. The mock-Tudor buildings on the right are modern, probably pre-dating this photograph by only one or two years.

THE CLOSE HOTEL, c. 1920. From 1875 the Close was the home of the solicitor Josiah Tippetts Paul. It became a hotel in the middle of this century.

TETBURY FLOWER SHOW AND CARNIVAL in Long Street, c. 1903. In the centre, coming along the street is the Holborow & Son float, shown in detail on page 61.

LONG STREET, c. 1900. J.W. Gardner, ironmonger and manufacturer, hot and cold water engineer, is seen on the immediate left of picture.

THE TOP OF LONG STREET, c. 1930.

THE TOP OF LONG STREET, *c.* 1900. This is one of a series of four photographs taken for Frith's postcard series at the turn of the century. The children have been posed for the pictures. The one boy in this picture would not be able to stand in the middle of the road today! Prout's Stores later became the Midland Bank: see the page opposite and notice the different façade.

THE MARKET PLACE: two more postcards in the 1900 Frith's series. The bottom picture was used for the cover of this book; note how the photographer used the early afternoon sunlight from the Church Street direction to highlight the gas lamp and the children. No doubt he gave the children a few coppers to encourage them to stay around. The top picture was taken at 12.20, the bottom one some fifty minutes later.

THE MARKET PLACE in two views thirty years apart. The top picture is the last of the Frith series, and dates from *c.* 1900. The bottom picture is from the Frank Packer series and, like those earlier in Long Street, dates from *c.* 1930. Packer was a photographer from Chipping Norton who did considerable work on the Cotswolds, but Tetbury was about the furthest point in his peripatetic travels.

SATTELY, JEWELLERS AND WATCHMAKERS, *c.* 1885. Wooden scaffolding is in place as the façade undergoes repair. This property stands next door to the Snooty Fox, (the White Hart).

TWO VIEWS OF THE MARKET PLACE, the top picture dating from *c.* 1890 and showing the same GWR sign as on the page opposite. The bottom picture is approximately thirty years later. There are no major structural differences, many minor points of detail (not least of which is the condition of the road) being all that goes to show the passing of one-third of a century.

THE TALBOT HOTEL, with the licensee and proprietor, 'Captain' Edwin Webb (captain of the Tetbury Fire Brigade), standing at the door.

TWO VIEWS AT THE TOP OF GUMSTOOL HILL, the top picture dating from *c.* 1907, the bottom picture *c.* 1930. In the bottom picture note the original telephone box; those were the days of real telephone kiosks, not the nasty plastic things we are getting today. There are many other minor points of difference, like the odd missing chimney-pot and the render having been removed from the house on the right-hand side, but essentially there has been little change in twenty years.

UNION STREET, c. 1907. The Union Workhouse stood on the right-hand side of this street. It was originally built about 1735, rebuilt in 1790, and following the Poor Law Act of 1834 became the Union Workhouse. It was demolished and rebuilt yet again in 1905–6, after which it became Cotswold Hospital maternity home until its recent closure. Union Street has now reverted to its earlier name of Gumstool Hill.

SILVER STREET, at its junction with the Green, c. 1890. The house on the right was the Three Compasses and in the middle is Bamford House, with Gordon House left of that. To the extreme left of picture is the Crown in Gumstool Hill.

TUGWELL'S DAINTY, 1903. Dainty was a champion pony of considerable fame in the area, bred by Richard Tugwell and eventually sold to a breeder in America. Pictured here on the Green.

FOX HILL looking down to Wiltshire Bridge, c. 1930.

WILTSHIRE BRIDGE AND THE STATION ENTRANCE, *c.* 1900.
Wiltshire (or Long) Bridge was built as a causeway to reduce the gradient. The original causeway was in existence by 1594, and presumably rebuilt when the Malmesbury Road was turnpiked in 1756. The causeway at one time marked the boundary between Gloucestershire and Wiltshire, with each county being responsible for the maintenance of its respective half.

TETBURY FROM MARSHALL'S HILL, *c.* 1920. A bleak winter scene, looking across to Wiltshire Bridge and Fox Hill.

WILTSHIRE BRIDGE AND FOX HILL, *c.* 1910. A view looking towards the town from the Malmesbury Road. Note the telegraph poles have now made their appearance; they do not appear on the page opposite.

THE COMING OF THE RAILWAY: the valley *c.* 1885 before work commences on the Tetbury branch, with the rope walk in the centre, and the Royal Oak visible in the distance.

TETBURY STATION STAFF, 1910. The familiar row of trees can be seen on the bank behind.

TETBURY STATION, *c.* 1910. Great celebrations accompanied the opening of the branch line on 2 December 1889. Tetbury was very late in getting its station – Dursley had a branch as early as 1856, Nailsworth in 1867 – but whereas the Dursley line was only two-and-a-half miles and Nailsworth four miles, the Tetbury branch required a line of seven miles. The line continued in use until the Beeching axe destroyed one of Britain's greatest assets – the branch railways. This British sickness of shortsightedness resulted in the Tetbury branch finally closing on 4 April 1964.

A SUNDAY SCHOOL OUTING from Tetbury Station, *c.* 1915. I may be wrong, but this has all the hallmarks of the annual Sunday School outing to Weston-super-Mare. In my own childhood in the 1950s and early 1960s I remember the annual trips to Weston, in the 1950s by train, later by coach; but my childhood trips were from Dursley station to Coaley Junction, and then on the direct line through Bristol and on to Weston. From Tetbury it must have been a major expedition. From Tetbury to Kemble, from Kemble to Swindon, from Swindon through to Temple Meads at Bristol, and then change again for Weston: this and back all in one day!

CHARLES JONES, haulier and licensee of the Royal Oak, standing beside a trailer pulled by his engine *King Edward*. The Royal Oak is in the background.

TETBURY FROM CIRENCESTER ROAD. This picture was on a postcard dated 1904. It was probably taken some time before, *c.* 1900. The Royal Oak is on the left and the old 1790 workhouse is just visible towards the top of Gumstool Hill.

TETBURY FROM CIRENCESTER ROAD. This picture was on a postcard dated 1904. It was probably taken some time before, *c.* 1900. The Royal Oak is on the left and the old 1836 workhouse is just visible towards the top of Gumstool Hill.

THE CHIPPING STEPS, *c.* 1930. The steps are one of the most photographed features of Tetbury. This photograph by Frank Packer of Chipping Norton is more unusual than most as it captures the steps from the top.

THE CHIPPING STEPS, *c.* 1885. This classic photograph has been attributed to the 1880s. The windows on the left are still of the lattice type, whereas in a picture that can be safely dated to 1905 they have been replaced by wooden casements. The picture has obviously been posed, and the photographer deserves some credit for this, bearing in mind the length of exposures at this time. This picture was used for many years afterwards on postcards by the Cotswold Publishing Company.

GREVILLE HILL, dairyman, in the Chipping, *c.* 1930.

THE CHIPPING, *c.* 1920, with Gloucester House in the centre. The house to the left of the large tree is the Priory, built in 1766 on the site of the old manor which had gone by 1594. Some of the cellars in the Priory still remain from the manor-house and are certainly medieval.

TWO VIEWS OF OCCASIONS IN THE CHIPPING. The top picture shows a military gathering *c.* 1907, possibly a recruiting party. The bottom picture may be on carnival day, *c.* 1910.

THE CONGREGATIONAL CHURCH, c. 1890. When the church was built in 1862, a large tree stood in front. The minister approached the feoffees seeking permission to fell the tree, but this was refused. However, the hand of God intervened: a few years later a great gale blew the tree down.

THE CHIPPING, c. 1905. A postcard was made out of this view in which the lady was 'painted out', presumably to give the image a longer life than would otherwise have been possible with changing fashions.

THE CORONATION DINNER AT TETBURY FOR KING EDWARD VII. The king wanted his coronation to be an occasion of national rejoicing, and in order that it should not be overshadowed by the Boer War it was not scheduled until the end was in sight and victory assured. 26 June 1902 was the date chosen.

On 14 June Edward was taken seriously ill with stomach pains and the coronation had to be postponed while he underwent an operation for appendicitis. Presumably the good people of Tetbury had already ordered the provisions, and in June 1902 they celebrated the king's recovery instead.

Detailed enlargements of this picture are shown on pages 2, 6 and 10.

CHURCH STREET at the junction with the Market Place, *c.* 1900. On the left is the Boot; towards the right, the Jolly Butchers.

CHURCH STREET from the opposite direction, looking into the Market Place, *c.* 1930. This picture was presumably taken on the same day as the view on page 25.

TWO VIEWS OF CHURCH STREET taken by Frank Packer *c.* 1934. The bottom picture shows a sign on the right-hand side, 'Tugwell Outfitter' next to the Eight Bells Inn.

THE TUGWELL FLYING MACHINE, *c.* 1908. In the doorway are, from left to right, Helena, Donald and Annie Tugwell and the boy on the tricycle is Ewart Tugwell, presumably before his departure to the carnival. The building on the right is the Eight Bells Inn.

CHURCH STREET, the top picture *c.* 1920, the bottom picture *c.* 1928, showing Persis Lamb's shop. Persis and her father, E.T. Lamb, took many of the pictures of Tetbury used in this book.

MR. RUDDER, COBBLER, standing at the top of Church Street, *c.* 1900. The Jolly Butchers Inn is on the right-hand side.

PASSING THE TIME OF DAY: an enlargement from the page opposite.

CHURCH STREET showing the original Three Cups, then occupied by Mr 'Trooper' Witchell, ironmonger, *c.* 1946.

BATH BRIDGE, C. 1900, showing the old road behind the cottage, leading to the old packhorse bridge.

BATH BRIDGE, *c.* 1910. This picture is taken from a Cotswold Publishing Company postcard, printed in collotype. Unfortunately the collotype printing has made the image rather too soft, losing some detail. Notice the group of children, a nice touch in the composition of the picture.

BATH BRIDGE, *c.* 1930, with Warn's Brewery chimney in the background. Bath Bridge was built by Thomas Webb in 1775 on behalf of the turnpike commissioners.

A VIEW OF BATH BRIDGE AND THE TOWN from Grange Fields, *c.* 1920.

HARPER STREET, *c.* 1900. The original name of this street was Hatter's Street. At the beginning of this century, Harper Street was the poor end of town. The name was later changed to West Street.

WEST STREET, *c.* 1930.

WEST STREET or, as it was then called, Harper Street, *c.* 1905.

CUTWELL HILL, C. 1905, with a detail enlargement.

CUTWELL. The top picture *c.* 1900, the bottom picture of 'Cutwell Docks' taken some fifteen or so years later. By this time a rail had been positioned alongside the bridge. The original bridge here dates from 1622 or earlier, when this route formed one of the main roads into the town. The top picture shows a Warn's Brewery cart; the bottom picture shows Kitty and Dorothy Price in a market cart.

TETBURY HAYMAKING, the Price family at work, from left to right: Eve, Tom, Mabel, Sybil, a visitor, Dennis, Ellen, Tom Cannon and another visitor.

TETBURY CHURCH AND BATH ROAD ARCHES from Cutwell, *c.* 1910.

BRINGING IN THE HAY, Dennis Price, two boys and two antipodean helpers, presumably Australians earning a few bob whilst on leave from Leighterton, or from the Australian transport section based in Tetbury at a garage at the end of Bath Bridge.

A TETBURY VICTORIAN FAMILY GROUP, c. 1880. A splendid picture, at a time when whiskers and conservatories were in vogue. If one did not know better, father and mother could have been Alfred Marks and Walter Matthau. Unfortunately, the real family are unknown.

TETBURY BAND, c. 1920.

HOLBOROW & SON, c. 1903. The float at the Tetbury Flower Show. This is probably the same float as shown in Long Street on page 21. Edward Holborow is in the centre of the picture.

INSIDE E.T. LAMB'S STUDIO IN CHURCH STREET, *c.* 1895. Edward J. Holborow and family pose in front of painted props. The boys are enjoying themselves, but mother is rather hesitant.

PHILLIPS & SONS, the float for the flower show and carnival, *c.* 1912. From left to right: Annie Cull, Harry Phillips, Mrs Phillips, Jack Phillips and two staff.

SECTION TWO

Nailsworth

THE HUNTER'S HALL, KINGSCOTE. Two views from the first decade of this century. The pictures were taken several years apart, to judge from the different forms of foliate growth on the front.

KINGSCOTE POST OFFICE, *c.* 1910.

HORSLEY, looking down the street, with the school on the right-hand side, *c.* 1955

THE BELL & CASTLE, HORSLEY. A view looking up the street, *c.* 1912.

DOWNEND, HORSLEY, *c.* 1900, looking towards Sugley Farm.

WASHPOOL, HORSLEY, *c.* 1895.

WHITEWAY, HORSLEY, *c.* 1910; Horsley Bridge with Downend in the background.

THE MIDLAND FISHERIES on the Horsley Stream, *c.* 1920.

MILL BOTTOM FROM THE BRISTOL ROAD, *c.* 1920, with Rockness above.

NAILSWORTH FROM ROCKNESS, *c*. 1905, with the oast houses of the brewery on the right-hand side. The pool shown centre left is Johnson's mill pond, later to become the town swimming pool.

THE SWIMMING POOL *c*. 1930. The pool was unchlorinated fresh water and always icy cold, the fresh water being constantly supplied from springs. At this time the town even had its own water polo team, but the pool fell out of use in the later 1930s.

ROCKNESS HOUSE, with Joseph Clissold junior standing in the gateway, wearing top hat and frock coat, and looking back up at the house. In the distance the Pepperpot Chapel, and between the gateway and the chapel it is possible to make out the wooden bridge which spanned Pike Lane.

This photograph is one of the oldest in this book, probably dating between 1865 and 1870, and is one of a pair, which together, viewed through the correct apparatus, gave a stereoscopic image – a popular medium in the Victorian age.

SHORTWOOD *c.* 1937, with All Saints Church on the left horizon, and Baptist school, now demolished, on the right.

OLD SHORTWOOD CHAPEL *c.* 1875. The house on the left was the Shortwood Baptist School and the stone from this was later used to build the Anglican church at Box.

OLD SHORTWOOD CHAPEL, seen here *c.* 1880, was built in 1838 to seat 1200, replacing an earlier chapel on the same site. It was dismantled in 1881 and the materials taken nearer to Nailsworth to rebuild it in Newmarket Road in the same year.

SHORTWOOD BAPTIST SCHOOL *c.* 1865. This fascinating, and extremely early, photograph is of great social interest. The Shortwood community was of considerable importance, being the largest Baptist community outside London. The Baptist Infants School was started in 1853 and continued for 90 years. This photograph shows some curious garb, although it is noteworthy that all of the children are shod, even though this is only thirty years after the economic collapse in the area at the failure of the woollen industry. Presumably the strong revival in the trade in 1848 more than balanced the earlier deprivation suffered by weavers and other cloth industry workers in the valleys.

SHORTWOOD BAPTIST INFANTS SCHOOL *c.* 1910. These two pictures are much later than the view on the facing page and show Miss Wilkins, the beloved 'Teacher', with her children. Single-handedly, she carried on at the school for thirty-six years.

NEWMARKET looking towards the High Wood, showing the now demolished cottages and the chimney of the Nodes Mill.

THE OLD NODES MILL with the Nodes House on the right-hand side, *c.* 1870. The Nodes House was built for Peter Hillier, Isaac Hillier's son, who was killed in a pony and trap accident in London in 1868. Isaac's original factory can be seen in the distance on the left-hand side.

LOOKING TOWARDS BUNTING HILL with the Nodes House in the centre, *c.* 1910.

NEWMARKET ROAD, built by Isaac Hillier to be wide enough for two pig carts to pass! The road was walled at this time on both sides.

HILLIER'S NEWMARKET COMPLEX *c.* 1880. At this time the factory was built around cottages as this picture shows.

NEWMARKET *c.* 1905. This view is much the same as the picture above, although changes are noticeable on the Hillier's site. Note the relative absence of trees in both photographs.

A VIEW OF NEWMARKET ROAD from the Bath Road *c.* 1900. The new Shortwood Baptist Chapel is clearly visible in the centre, with Worley top left-hand side, and Chestnut Hill in the top right.

LAYING THE FOUNDATION STONE. The old chapel in Shortwood was dismantled in 1881, and the materials were brought into Nailsworth for rebuilding in Newmarket Road. The foundation stone was laid on Thursday 16 June 1881 amidst a continuous downfall of rain, the ceremony being conducted under umbrellas. A contemporary report recorded that 'A continuous downpour of rain greatly interfered with the attendances and the comfort of those present.'

This view was taken from behind Price's Mill, with the mill chimney and buildings to the left of the picture.

CHESTNUT HILL HOUSE, with the Deverells to the top right. The new chapel can be seen on the extreme left.

THE NEWMARKET VALLEY, with the new Shortwood Chapel in the centre and Chestnut Hill behind, *c.* 1890.

THE NEWMARKET VALLEY *c.* 1905, in a similar view to that on the previous page, but this picture shows the new church parlour and caretaker's house, as well as much additional detail in the background. Another interesting point of comparison is the difference in focal length between the two pictures. Both are taken from more or less the same spot, behind larch trees, and yet this picture enhances the foreground.

It may seem that the Shortwood Chapel is being given over-exposure in this book. In fact the Shortwood Community was of major importance in the development of Nailsworth and a strange but desirable social situation where, unlike the Anglican 'establishment', employer and employee sat side by side. Mill owner and weaver shared the office of deacons. Until 1894 when Nailsworth finally became a parish, the Baptists were responsible in a voluntary and unofficial capacity for many of the social and educational activities in the town.

Since 1969 the chapel has been Christ Church, Nailsworth – a reunion of the nonconformists after 250 years as separate denominations.

THE CHAPEL WITH THE NEW CHURCH PARLOUR AND CARETAKER'S HOUSE 1905. The little boy is my grandfather, Harold Mayo, with his father, my great-grandfather, Arthur, who was the caretaker at that time.

A SUNDAY SCHOOL CLASS, 1905, outside the church parlour. The little boy front, left, is the same as in the picture above.

LOOKING ACROSS THE NEWMARKET VALLEY TO THE TOWN. This view is from Worley looking across the chapel roof to the town, with Price's Mill chimney on the right-hand side. The photograph must be c. 1900 as the new parish church is just visible by the gas lamp on the left-hand side of the picture.

INCHBROOK CHURCH 1925. This quaint iron church was built in 1850.

NAILSWORTH INFANTS WELFARE GROUP, *c.* 1915.

A FIRST WORLD WAR NAILSWORTH CONTINGENT. Little is known about this picture. It is obviously First World War, but the men themselves and exactly where they are standing have not been identified. They appear to be officers and NCOs.

THE NAILSWORTH WARDENS, 1943.

THE NAILSWORTH & WOODCHESTER VALLEY VOLUNTEER FIRE BRIGADE, which took responsibility for tackling fires in the valleys until 1940 when it was incorporated in the County Council service. This fire engine was acquired in 1924, probably converted from a First World War army surplus vehicle. The photograph was probably taken *c.* 1935.

THE PROCLAMATION OF KING GEORGE V, outside the Subscription Rooms, 16 May 1910.

A TEA PARTY AT THE BANNUT TREE HOUSE, *c.* 1905. This is an interesting picture: because of the length of exposure, it must have been posed. Miss Tabram of the Bannut (Walnut) Tree House probably has her arm on a photographers 'prop rest', invisible to the camera, so that it appears quite natural when she is pouring the tea. The give-away is the maid's apron which is gently blowing in the breeze, showing that the exposure must have been several seconds at the very least.

TWENTY-FIVE YEARS LATER – the Silver Jubilee of King George V, May 1935. This picture taken at the entrance to Old Market, with Olive Vick, Mary Davis and Molly Timbrell.

A VIEW ACROSS TO WATLEDGE, with Shears Pitch in the centre distance. Arnold's Lane is on the right-hand side and the brewery on the right in the distance. This photograph c. 1896.

LOOKING DOWN THE BATH ROAD, with the Pepperpot Church in the distance, c. 1896.

THE CROSS, 1870. The Bath Road is very narrow at this time. The man standing outside the ironmonger's shop is the proprietor, Samuel Newman. He was the co-founder with Francis Joseph Hender of Newman Hender & Co. Ltd.

THE OPPOSITE VIEW, *c.* 1880. This view is the exact opposite of the picture above, showing the Pepperpot Chapel and Fountain Street.

THE PEPPERPOT CHAPEL, showing the full extent of the Anglican chapel, built in 1794 to the design of Nathaniel Dyer and demolished in 1898 to make way for the new parish church. A great shame, as the Pepperpot had character. An interesting point to note is the photographer's licence. He has painted out the telegraph pole that stood on the corner (see page 90). In this picture the wires float in the air.

At this period Fountain Street was a dead end. Day's Mill went right across the street and the through route was behind the church. Day's Mill was truncated towards the end of the century, allowing the through route that we know today.

This picture dates to c. 1870. Some of the brick buildings in Fountain Street have not yet been built. The large tree in the churchyard was presumably cut down shortly after as it does not feature in the picture on page 90.

THE CROSS, c. 1910, with the King's Head and the Crown virtually opposite each other looking down Market Street.

FOUNTAIN STREET, 1938. The wooden clock tower was donated by Mr W.G. Clissold to house the clock, and also the Rudhall bells which dated back to 1795, until such time as a church tower was built. This never actually occurred and the wooden tower was sadly demolished in 1952, being replaced by the new tower further down.

W.H. SMITH'S NAILSWORTH BRANCH, *c.* 1945, with Miss Dorothy Marshall standing in the doorway.

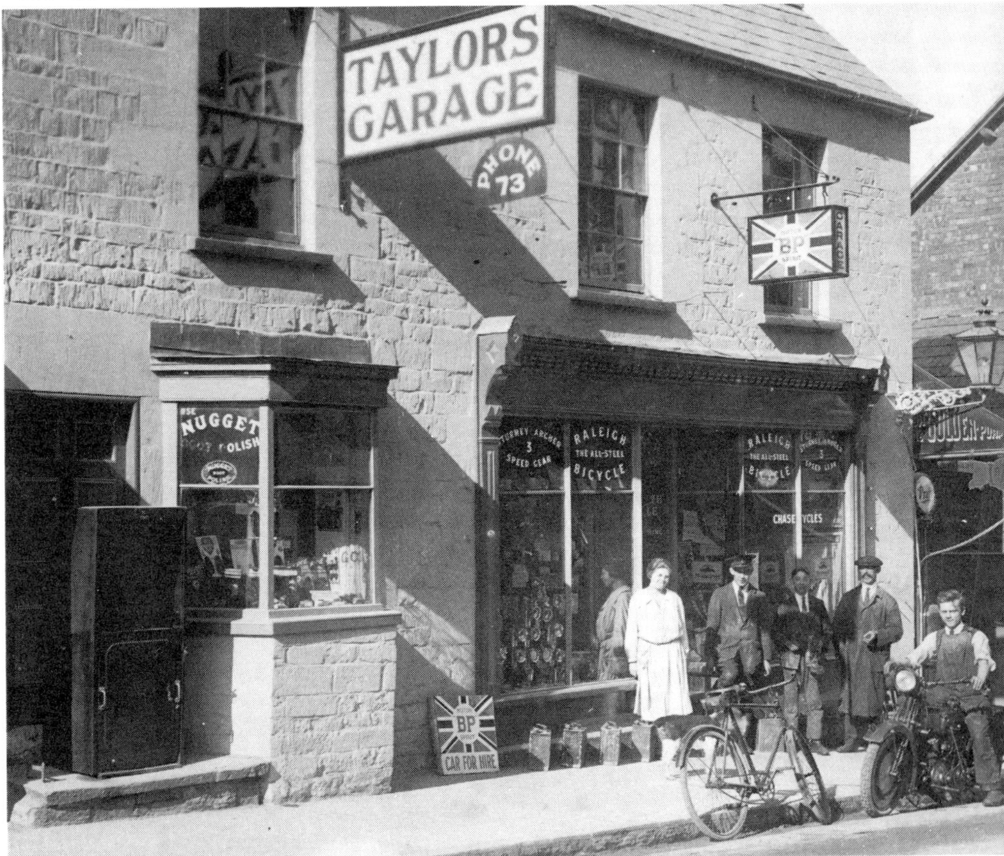

TAYLOR'S GARAGE, Foutain Street, c. 1928, advertising Sturmey Archer 3-speed gears, Raleigh bicycles and Pratt's Motor Spirit – amongst other things. This property was demolished and the site is now covered by the Mortimer Gardens.

FOUNTAIN STREET from outside Lloyd's Bank, *c.* 1958.

FOUNTAIN STREET AND BRIDGE STREET, in 1938. The clue to this date is the wall poster on the right-hand side, advertising a horse show on Saturday 4 September. The only Saturday 4 September that matches with the cars and the clothing style is 1938.

MARKET STREET from the direction of the Cross, *c.* 1885.

MARKET STREET from the direction of Cossack Square, *c.* 1885.

MARKET STREET from Cossack Square, *c.* 1875, showing the brick houses in the distance in the latter stages of construction. Before the railway came to Nailsworth, virtually no buildings were constructed of brick.

MARKET STREET AND BUTCHER HILL'S LANE, *c.* 1910.

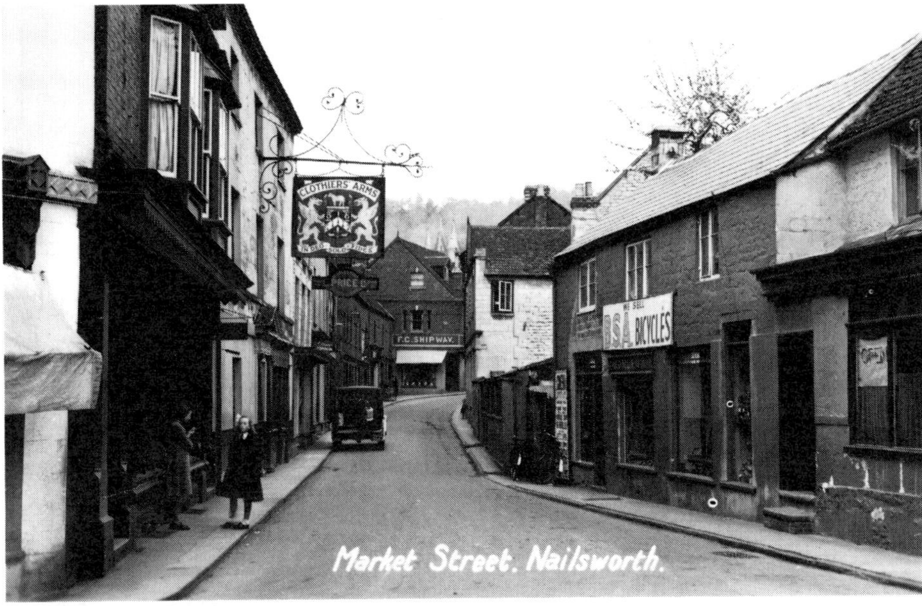

TWO VIEWS OF MARKET STREET, both much more modern than the previous pictures. There are some clues for dating. The top picture looks 'cleaner', but I believe it to be the older of the two photographs. To begin with, the schoolgirls look *c.* 1947, whereas in the bottom picture the lady's hat is early 1950s, possibly *c.* 1954. The final clues are the 'no waiting' sign on the right-hand side and the telephone wire crossing above the street.

MR WALL'S HAT, CAP & GENERAL WAREHOUSE IN MARKET STREET, C. 1890. The buildings on the left were demolished in the 1950s.

BUTCHER HILL'S LANE, c. 1865. This is one of the oldest photographs in this book. Note the differences between this picture and the facing view of about twenty years later. To begin with, there are no houses in the background; the corner of the Red Lion Inn on the right-hand side, one starts 'Red', the other looks as if it starts 'The'; the first house on the left has a smaller window with a shutter. Finally (although there are numerous other clues if the pictures are studied enough), this picture has a bracket for a removable oil lamp, while the right-hand picture has a gas lamp – gas was supplied to Nailsworth streets in 1876.

BUTCHER HILL'S LANE, c. 1885.

TWO PICTURES OF COSSACK SQUARE. The top view is *c.* 1948, the bottom view *c.* 1960.

Established 1790.

W. J. WHITING,

Wholesale and Family ...

GROCER, TEA and PROVISION MERCHANT.

WINES and SPIRITS.

Huntley and Palmer's Biscuits.
Coffee a Speciality—Freshly Roasted on the premises.

THE OLD STAMP OFFICE,

NAILSWORTH.

W.J. WHITING's ADVERTISEMENT from the *Stroud Valley Illustrated*, published by Burrow's in 1903.

STAR HILL AND THE FOREST GREEN CHAPEL, *c.* 1935. This was the second chapel to be built on the site. Erected in 1872, it was demolished in 1946.

WINSLOW HOUSE, SPRING HILL. Originally Springhill House, later the Lawn, now Winslow House. It was here that the real 'Winslow Boy' lived, except his name was not Winslow, it was Archer-Shea. He was accused of stealing money from a fellow pupil at college and his father engaged a noted lawyer to defend him. This was a major *cause célèbre* at the beginning of the century and was later made into a play by Terence Rattigan and a film in 1949, starring Robert Donat, Margaret Leighton and Cedric Hardwicke. The real boy was killed in the First World War.

CHURCH STREET 1902, decorated for the coronation of King Edward VII.

GEORGE STREET, *c.* 1900, with three young Nailsworth citizens studying the photographer from outside Waterloo House, now the Midland Bank.

.. Waterloo House, NAILSWORTH.

John Morris

and SONS,

Family Drapers and Gent.'s Outfitters,
Costumes, Mantles, Jackets, Millinery.

Always a large and well-assorted stock of Drapery Goods, Household Linens, Beddings, Lace Curtains, Carpet Squares, Linoleums, Hearth Rugs, Etc.

Our Dressmaking Department receives most careful supervision, and Ladies can always rely on obtaining the Newest Styles and Good Fit at most reasonable charges.

Mourning and Wedding orders executed at short notice.
Funerals Completely Furnished. Estimates given.

Gent.'s and Boys' Clothing of every description.
Bespoke Suits, Trousers, Overcoats, Etc., made to measure.

Boots and Shoes of every description.

JOHN MORRIS & SONS, **Waterloo House, .. NAILSWORTH.**

JOHN MORRIS & SONS from the *Stroud Valley Illustrated*, 1903.

THE FOUNTAIN which gave the name to Fountain Street. It was erected here in 1862 and subsequently moved to its present position. This picture of the end of Fountain Street and of Bridge Street was taken *c.* 1870.

BRIDGE STREET, *c.* 1948. This modern picture was taken from a similar position to that above. The wool shop was still in existence; altogether it must have clocked up close to a hundred years under different owners.

THE FOUNTAIN, c. 1880. Sadly this picture was very faded and the overall effect is one of greyness.

DAUNCEY'S SHOP FRONTS decorated for the coronation of King Edward VII in 1902.

THE BERLIN WOOL AND FANCY REPOSITORY, *c.* 1900, in this picture under the ownership of Redmans. Berlin wool, named after the German capital, was the usual name for ordinary knitting wool. The term, which had been in use for over a hundred years, fell out of use around the time of the First World War.

C. J. DAUNCEY,

Hosier, Hatter and Outfitter,

1 and 2, Bridge Street, NAILSWORTH, Glos.

The Noted House for..

'Ardwear' Boots and Shoes.

New Crown Strap Leggings and Gaiters,

Fox's New Patent

PUTTEES.

Jaeger Pure Wool Underwear.

Agent for the celebrated

Cellular Clothing.

The Newest and Up-to-date Novelties in

Men's, Youths', Boys' and Juvenile Wear.

BRITISH SPORTS.

Cricket, Lawn Tennis, Golf, Football, Hockey, Gymnasia,

and all..

Outdoor and Indoor Games.

C.J. DAUNCEY, an advertisement from the *Stroud Valley Illustrated*, 1903.

THE STATION ENTRANCE FROM BRIDGE STREET, *c.* 1870.

THE NAILSWORTH TERMINUS, *c.* 1905. The railway came late to Nailsworth. The line was opened in 1867, but became an early closure casualty, being closed to passenger traffic in 1947 and to goods in 1966.

BRIDGE STREET AND THE GREAT STORM. I have not been able to identify when this storm occurred, but judging from the costume, and by the original photograph I was lucky enough to borrow, printed in sepia on very thin photograpic paper, the date must be in the early 1880s. The horse chestnut tree on the right-hand side, just this side of the railway hotel, has certainly grown much larger, but apart from this there are no further clues. Looking at the damage, the storm must have been severe. The photograph was taken from Bridge Street, looking across at the station entrance, with the coal yards on the left.

WATLEDGE, c. 1910, with Yatesfield centre left.

WATLEDGE, c. 1900. The railway is in the foreground, although mainly hidden by trees. In the centre, some railway carriages are just visible.

A VIEW FROM NAILSWORTH HILL, *c.* 1910.

LOOKING TOWARDS THE PARISH CHURCH, *c.* 1900. The temporary 'iron' church is clearly visible on the left hand side.

NAILSWORTH FROM SHEARS PITCH, *c.* 1900. This photograph is looking across the top of Watledge, with the station yard and railway on the right of the picture, and Day's Mill and the new church in the centre.

NAILSWORTH FROM THE 'W', *c.* 1900, the top picture showing the town, the bottom picture looking over Worley, Chestnut Hill and Forest Green. Note the lack of development at this time and the relative paucity of trees.

DUNKIRK MILLS, INCHBROOK. Built by the Playne family around 1780 as a factory mill for the woollen trade, Dunkirk Mill ceased manufacturing cloth sometime before 1891, when it was used for the manufacture of hosiery. This was short-lived and by 1903 it had become Walker's walking stick factory.

NAILSWORTH BREWERY, a rather fanciful drawing, possibly used as a letterhead for the company. Founded in 1820 by Ann Overbury, the brewery was one of the largest employers in the area for most of the nineteenth century.

THE DEVIL'S ELBOW: two views of Holcombe Woods, *c.* 1910.

LONGFORD'S MILL AND HOUSE, *c.* 1920. The original part of the house (the western wing) was built *c.* 1800 by William Playne. The mill had already been in business since the eighteenth century, but was greatly enlarged in 1912.

LONGFORD'S HOUSE, the east view from the terrace. This view of 1914 was published in *A History of the Parishes of Minchinhampton and Avening*, by Arthur Twisden Playne, 1915.

LONGFORD'S LAKE, *c.* 1910. The lake was built in 1806 to create a back-up water supply to the mill, which, although fitted with steam engines, still required considerable water power. During the riots of 1824 and 1825, the dam was guarded day and night to prevent rioters breaching it and flooding the valley. The top picture shows Longford's House top left, and the bottom picture shows the boathouse.

LONGFORD'S MILL 1914. The top picture shows the weaving sheds, the bottom picture shows the spinning mill. This factory had been built just two years before.

SECTION THREE

Minchinhampton

THE NAILSWORTH TO AVENING BUS at Avening *c.* 1907. The bus was a Thornycroft operated by Arnolds of Nailsworth. The driver was one of the Arnolds family.

AVENING, *c.* 1900. The Bell and the lower end of High Street.

AVENING, the lower end of High Street, 1902.

AVENING, High Street and Point Road from Rectory Lane, *c.* 1905.

A VIEW OF AVENING from Paradise, *c.* 1905.

AVENING AND MINCHINHAMPTON HILL, c. 1900.

THE OLD SCHOOL, MINCHINHAMPTON. The school was built on the site of an old manor house and opened in April 1868. This picture may be showing part of the opening celebrations, which included a parade of children through the town.

THE OLD SCHOOL, this time about forty years later, when the building had had time to mature. Note the tall bushes where the pupils were photographed in the top picture. The school was destined to last one hundred years, being demolished around 1968.

MINCHINHAMPTON FOOTBALL TEAM c. 1905.

ROGERS & SONS Noah's Ark & Dodgems *c.* 1920 when the traction engines were new.

MINCHINHAMPTON TOWN BAND 1903.

PEA PICKING AT HAMPTON FIELDS *c.* 1920. The original of this picture is unfortunately badly damaged.

GATCOMBE LODGE before 1914.

GATCOMBE PARK, built by Edward Sheppard, 1771–4 and now the home of the Princess Royal. In the early nineteenth century it was the home of David Ricardo, described by William Cobbett in his *Rural Rides* as 'a boroughmonger, of all God's creatures, the basest . . . '

WEST END looking away from the town, with the Swan Inn, centre, *c.* 1910.

WEST END again, probably about the same date as above. The Swan is still visible, centre distance.

FRIDAY STREET looking towards the town, *c.* 1905.

RECTORY COTTAGE AND THE COIGNE *c.* 1903. Butt Street is centre distance, the Coigne is on the right. This was once the old rectory and is now a private house. This wide area was once the site of Upper Island, one of the three Minchinhampton market houses, which was demolished in the middle of the last century.

THE CORNER OF HIGH STREET, LOOKING INTO TETBURY STREET *c.* 1955, showing the Salutation on the right-hand side.

THE SAME VIEW, but this picture is much older, probably *c.* 1920, and shows more of the bottom of High Street at this period, including the White Hart.

WEST END looking towards the Cross and Tetbury Street from a position just outside of the Swan, *c.* 1905.

TELEPHONE 153 for your best quality English meat. A. Gabb, butcher, was at the end of West End. The same view, including London House, is shown on the next page.

OGDEN'S GENERAL DRAPERY at the Cross, before the First World War.

This detail from the picture on page 142 shows Ogden's Drapery and Outfitting Stores some fifteen years or so later.

WELL HILL LOOKING INTO HIGH STREET *c*. 1938.

BOVRIL

H WALKER
Shell
BP

Above:

BAPTIST WHITSUN SUNDAY SCHOOL TREAT 1907. Looking up High Street on the left-hand side we can see several changes. Walker's bottom shop was then G.A. Benjamin, family grocer, and the top shop of the 1930s did not then have the projecting shop front. The shop in the bottom left-hand corner of the picture had two attractive bays, but these had been replaced by a more austere frontage by the 1930s.

Top left: At a risk of overdoing High Street in the 1930s, this fine detailed picture was too good to resist including. It is winter, probably *c.* 1932, and the Virginia creeper is in its normal winter leafless state. One lady is kindly standing still for us, gossiping to someone out of the picture, and we therefore have her costume to help in dating. Another figure is rushing down the street, much faster than the slow exposure of the camera can cope with, and is subsequently a blur to posterity. The top of Walker's stores looks as if it was built in fine ashlar, but looks deceive, and really it was just render, with lines being drawn whilst still wet. This render has now been removed to show a Cotswold stone rubble construction.

Bottom left: A detailed shot of Walker's Stores, *c.* 1939. The sign on the fence reads 'BP fill your car here'. The picture is probably pre-war as no rationing signs are in evidence.

HILLIER & CO. STATIONER AND FANCY GOODS. This picture is a more direct view of the same shop, shown on the previous page to the left of the picture. This view is very slightly later, possibly 1908. The only noticeable difference is the appearance of the advertisements for Fry's chocolate in the windows. Mrs Hillier is standing in the doorway with her daughter Mabel.

HIGH STREET *c.* 1905. A lady is standing in the doorway of Sommer's sweet shop, a boy is lounging against the window and the grocer (Mr Hughes?) is standing in the doorway of Hughes' Grocery Store. Under the 'L' of 'Crown Hotel', a man is standing watching the photographer, whilst behind him to his right is a traveller with a bag on a stick over his shoulder. To the right is Lower Island, demolished some years later to make way for the war memorial.

THE MARKET SQUARE *c.* 1925, showing the newly constructed war memorial.

HIGH STREET looking towards the Cross. This fine quality picture shows a great deal of detail and an enlargement is given below. See also page 136. The enlargement below shows a building in what was once a passage way to a public house behind. The pub was possibly the Ten Bells. This building appeared towards the end of the last century.

LOWER ISLAND *c.* 1890, one of the three Minchinhampton market houses. The site is now covered by the war memorial.

THE MARKET SQUARE *c.* 1900, showing the Lower Island in the centre. The Ram is on the left-hand side; this has been a public house since at least the end of the seventeenth century. Until about 1750 it was known as the Pen and Hand, after which time it changed to the Ram.

THE SIGN OF THE RAM c. 1935.

TWO VIEWS OF TETBURY STREET. The top view is older, probably *c.* 1905, showing the old forge on the left-hand side, the post office on the right. The bottom picture with the children is later, probably *c.* 1919.

THE MARKET HOUSE *c.* 1925. This was built in 1698 to be the centre of a successful wool and yarn market, and what was then one of the four chief markets in the county. Over the next few years this situation changed dramatically as Tetbury took the lead in the wool trade. The market house has since been used for a variety of purposes right up to this day.

THE MARKET HOUSE *c.* 1935. A view, rather over-exposed, looking out into the market place.

LOWER ISLAND from the market place c. 1910. The Lower Island was also called the Old Institute. It was used as a rifle range, and for school cookery classes amongst other things. It was demolished to make way for the war memorial in 1919.

LOWER ISLAND from the market place c. 1910.

HIGH STREET AND WELL HILL from the church tower c. 1900.

FRIDAY STREET from the church tower c. 1925. The Coigne and Butt Street are to the bottom left. The first few houses on the right in Friday Street were demolished to make way for the present car park.

WELL HILL LOOKING DOWN TOWARDS THE ROYAL OAK c. 1905

A SHOP IN WELL HILL. These are probably the same ladies as in the picture above, on the right-hand side, standing outside their shop.

WELL HILL LOOKING UP TOWARDS TOWN c. 1905. Are these the same ladies again? I believe they are, and they are standing in the same doorway. Obviously photographers were points of interest. Little do these ladies realise that, through the photographer's art, they themselves have now become points of interest.

WELL HILL c. 1890. This is basically the same view as above, but I believe it is fifteen years or so earlier. Note the large hedge and the post and chain fencing, which has been replaced in the top picture. Although the detail is too small to easily discern, the gentleman standing with his hands on his hips is wearing a frock coat, more typical of the late nineteenth century, whereas the ladies in the top picture are most definitely Edwardian.

KING STREET c. 1900.

COFFIN HOUSE c. 1900. It was apparently named 'Coffin House' because of its shape; however, as the premises were once used by an undertaker, perhaps there was more substance to the name!

WELL HILL LOOKING TOWARDS FORWOOD, 1935. The house top right is Forwood House, now called Forwood Grange, and the cottage at the bottom of the hill is Fairview. Within the walled square at the bottom of the hill was hidden the town gasometer.

A VIEW BELOW WELL HILL, *c.* 1905. The Shard in its earlier form is to the right.

WELL HILL looking up towards town, *c*. 1935.

MINCHINHAMPTON FROM FORWOOD in 1907, with the Shard to the right.

MINCHINHAMPTON FROM FORWOOD some five or six years later. The Shard has now sprouted dormer windows. Note how few trees there are in these pictures compared with today.

THE SHARD c. 1935.

THE OLD LODGE GOLF CLUB HOUSE c. 1915. This picture was taken from the back of the house. Note the striped canvas awning, or is it, perhaps, something more substantial than canvas?

THE OLD LODGE, the same shot as above, this time approximately ten years later. The structure to the right is definitely more substantial now.

MINCHINHAMPTON COMMON AND THE OLD LODGE. This view from the Common of *c.* 1930 shows the splayed roof of the extension mentioned on the previous page. This structure has now (1988) disappeared.

THE HALFWAY HOUSE *c.* 1900.

TOM LONG'S POST *c.* 1925. Theories vary as to who Tom Long was. Suffice it to say that the present mile post is nowhere near as splendid as this structure.

TOM LONG'S POST *c.* 1935. This view looking towards Minchinhampton.

A VIEW FROM MINCHINHAMPTON COMMON, *c.* 1935. Looking over Burleigh and Beechknapp, with Quarhouse on the hill opposite, and Chalford Hill in the distance to the centre and right.

THE RAGGED COT. Date unknown, but judging from the light fitting to the top right of the door, it could be in the 1950s.

TWO QUARRY VIEWS. The top picture is believed to be Simmond's Quarry, and from the costume could be as late as the 1930s. The bottom picture is much older, probably the 1880s or 1890s.

A VIEW OF BOX FROM THE COMMON, c. 1915. Box Inn is in the centre. Note the haystacks in the foreground.

BOX, FROM THE SOUTH-EAST, c. 1920.

A VIEW OF BOX FROM THE GREEN, *c.* 1910.

BOX COMMUNITY MISSION CHURCH, *c.* 1930. This nonconformist meeting room was built about 1928, the pastor was Gregory Hopper. Behind the Community Mission Church is a radio aerial built by Mr Denley in 1925, and behind that is the roof-line of the three-gabled Beehive Inn.

PINFARTHINGS, c. 1905.

A SIMILAR PICTURE OF PINFARTHINGS, some twenty years later, with a good view over the valley to Forest Green.

GARDNER'S STORES, PINFARTHINGS, *c.* 1925. The cross is painted on the photograph, not on the roof! This view is looking over the Inchbrook Valley towards Woodchester, with Atcombe Wood in the distance.

THE AMBERLEY RIDGE PRIVATE HOTEL, *c.* 1910. Now the Amberley Ridge Special School.

THE AMBERLEY INN, c. 1905.

THE AMBERLEY INN, c. 1920. The inn has now been 'poshed up'. The charming vernacular buildings to the left of the inn shown in the top picture have been demolished, and the pseudo-Elizabethan Cotswold-style buildings have made their appearance, a style which now pervades both Rodborough and Minchinhampton commons.

ROSE COTTAGE, AMBERLEY, 1936. This was the cottage in which Mrs Craik (Dinah Mulock) wrote her novel, *John Halifax, Gentleman*, published in 1857. The hero, John Halifax, is an orphan boy who makes good by his own industry, the point of the story being that gentlemen are born, not made by claims of birth and wealth! The fabric of the novel is moulded very much from this area, including the Playne family of Longfords, and Dunkirk Mill.

ROSE COTTAGE in another view, looking down from the common.

A VIEW OF AMBERLEY in 1929. This picture is taken a little further from the inn. The elm in the middle has gone, but otherwise, although altered, virtually all the buildings shown are still standing. The whitewashed cottage has lost its wash, but back in the eighteenth and nineteenth centuries, most Cotswold stone cottages would have been whitewashed, and not the plain stone we know today.

THE AMBERLEY BAKERY, c. 1910.

THE SCHOOL, AMBERLEY, *c.* 1905. The foundation stone was laid on 20 June 1887 to commemorate Queen Victoria's Golden Jubilee. The green in front, to the south-west, has now gone up-market with pleached limes as in a French market square.

AMBERLEY, *c.* 1915. The scots pines have now grown until they almost hide the school from this same viewpoint. The name Amberley comes from a small hamlet south of Littleworth, but after the church and a school were built here in 1836, the name was extended to be the collective area name, and Littleworth is now 'little' used.

HOUNDSCROFT LOOKING TOWARDS BEARPOOLS, *c.* 1900.

THE ORIGINAL BEAR HOTEL. This picture was taken *c.* 1904 and shows the hotel before the major alterations and additions of the 1920s.

THE BEAR INN, *c.* 1895. Here in this picture the caption on the original postcard refers to the Bear as an 'inn'. When did it become a hotel?

THE BEAR INN, *c.* 1908. This is one of the last views before the drastic changes of the 1920s.

THE BEAR HOTEL GARDENS, *c.* 1905.

THE BEAR HOTEL GARDENS, *c.* 1930. Note the amazing differences; the structure might almost have been demolished and rebuilt for what went into the alterations.

BEAR TRANSMOGRIFICATION. This photograph of 1927 shows the result of adding a schloss, on to a pseudo-Cotswold wing, on to an existing, but much altered vernacular building of the late seventeenth century! Note the differences from the pictures on the preceding pages.

The following is an extract from the *Gloucester Journal* of 24 July 1750: '... The same Monday July 21st., a Ball of Fire fell on the Bear Inn in the Road to Hampton, which broke down Parts of the End of the House, took off the End of the Bedstead and Curtains of the Bed, where the man and his wife lay, then went thro' the Floor and made its Way thro' the Wall of the kitchen, however, by the Providence of God, they escaped all Hurt, tho' they were terribly affrighted. . . .'

The Prince and Princess of Wales and Lady Augusta, who were staying at Lord Bathurst's in Cirencester, passed the Bear that same day on their way to visit Mr Onesiphorus Paul at Woodchester: '. . . as he passed by the Bear Inn aforesaid on Monday, and was informed of the Damage the People sustained, he was graciously pleased to order them two Guineas.'

BEARPOOLS FROM THE ROAD OUTSIDE THE BEAR, *c.* 1908.

BEARPOOLS FROM ALMOST THE SAME POSITION AS ABOVE, *c.* 1930.

BEARPOOLS LOOKING TOWARDS THE BEAR, *c.* 1935.

A VIEW OF SOUTH WOODCHESTER from below St Chloe, *c.* 1905.

SOUTH WOODCHESTER, two views of *c.* 1912.

ACKNOWLEDGEMENTS

The compilation of this book has been made a great pleasure due to three people who have given time, encouragement and a great deal of support in helping me in my enquiries, and in lending pictures for reproduction; they Are Betty Mills, Ted Prince and Stanley Gardiner. Without their help, I could not have produced this book.

I would like to thank Mr Baker and Minchinhampton Primary School, the County Archivist and staff at Gloucestershire Record Office for their support and assistance, and also the the Oxfordshire County Museum at Woodstock. For individual contributions I wish to thank the following who have lent photographs, or have supplied information used in this book; Mr Peter Bristow, Mr Danny Drinkwater, Mr Donald Emes, Mr Michael Evans, Mr David Holborow, Mr A.J. Martin, Mr George Mills, Mr John Phillips, Miss Jean Price, Mr A.C. Turk and Mrs E. Tugwell.

I feel sure that I have missed thanking others who have helped. If so, this is inadvertant. I should also point out that errors and omissions are my responsibility alone. I would hope that the book is, by and large, accurate; but by the nature of a book such as this, there will be mistakes.

Finally, I would like to make a point of saying that the dates presented are mainly my opinions, and may in some cases be twenty years out! When accompanied by a 'circa', they are my interpretations. When without, they are dated with some certainty.

Alan Sutton.

GLOUCESTERSHIRE IN OLD PHOTOGRAPHS

1 **The Forest in Old Photographs**. Humphrey Phelps. ISBN 0 86299 078 5
2 **The Forest in Old Photographs – a Second Selection**. Humphrey Phelps. ISBN 086299 186 2
3 **The Forest in Old Photographs – from the Dean Heritage Museum Collection**. David Mullin. ISBN 086299 410 1
4 **Newent to Ross-on-Wye in Old Photographs.** ISBN 086299 438 1.
5 **Tewkesbury and the Vale of Gloucester in Old Photographs**. Charles Hilton. ISBN 086299 416 0
6 **Gloucester in Old Photographs**. Jill Voyce. ISBN 086299 258 3.
7 **Around Gloucester in Old Photographs**. Alan Sutton. ISBN 086299 400 4. *In preparation*.
8 **Cheltenham in Old Photographs**. Roger Whiting. ISBN 086299 276 1
9 **Cheltenham in Old Photographs – a Second Selection**. Roger Whiting. ISBN 086299 433 0.
10 **Bishop's Cleeve to Winchcombe in Old Photographs**. David H. Aldred. ISBN 086299 403 9
11 **The North Cotswolds in Old Photographs** David Viner. ISBN 086299 441 1.
12 **Northleach to Stow-on-the-Wold in Old Photographs**. David Viner. ISBN 086299 399 7
13 **Fairford and Lechlade in Old Photoraphs**. Edwin Cuss and Brian Rushby. ISBN 086299 390 3
14 **Cirencester in Old Photographs**. Jean Welsford. ISBN 086299 311 3
15 **Stroud and the Five Valleys in Old Photographs**. S.J. Gardiner and L.C. Padin. ISBN 086299 015 7
16 **Stroud and the Five Valleys in Old Photographs – a Second Selection**. S.J. Gardiner and L.C. Padin. ISBN 086299 465 5
17 **Stroud Valley Road and Rail in Old Photographs**. S.J. Gardiner and L.C. Padin. ISBN 086299 470 5
18 **Tetbury, Nailsworth and Minchinhampton in Old Photographs**. Alan Sutton. ISBN 086299 402 0
19 **Wotton-under-Edge to Chipping Sodbury in Old Photographs**. Alan Sutton. ISBN 086299 389 X
20 **Thornbury to Berkeley in Old Photographs**. John Hudson. ISBN 086299 388 1
21 **Around Dursley in Old Photographs**. Ann Wilson and David Evans. ISBN 086299 311 3
22 **Stonehouse to Painswick in Old Photographs**. Alan Sutton. ISBN 086299 401 2. *In preparation*.
23 **The Severn Vale in Old Photographs**. Alan Sutton. ISBN 0 86299 271 0